W9-BNT-966

Who has ascended into heaven, or descended? Who has gathered the wind in His fists? Who has bound the waters in a garment? Who has established all the ends of the earth? What is His name, and what is His Son's name, If you know? Proverbs 30:4

This book is available through:

Elisha Vision Publishing
P.O. Box 1601
Wake Forest, NC 27588

Or it can be ordered directly from www.ElishaVision.com

This book was printed in the USA by

InstantPublisher.com
P.O. Box 340, 410 Highway 72 W.
Collierville TN 38027

ISBN 978-0-9843958-6-6

SIMPLE ISLAM

Les Lawrence

Elisha Vision Publishing

Other books by Les Lawrence:

Prophecy to the Land

Generation LAST

Generation LIGHT

Generation LIFE

Books by Doreen Lawrence:

How Hanukkah Saved Christmas

A Lamb for Rachel

A Three Strand Cord

Dedication

This book is dedicated to Yehovah, the faithful God of the Bible. He is the only true God, the God of Israel, and He is the God of Abraham, Isaac, and Jacob.

And He LOVES Muslims so much that He sent His Son, Jesus (Yeshua) to die for them.

Acknowledgements

I am so thankful for my dear wife and best friend, Doreen. Her love is expressed over and over in the technical details, not only of the book, but living with me.

My brother, Ken, has personally hounded me (in the Spirit of the "Hound of Heaven") to write this particular book. Thank you, Ken, for your vision.

I am grateful for the final editing feedback from my valued friends, Sirus Chitsaz, Dale Suggs, and John Fisk. We also appreciate all the friends who have supported our Elisha Vision Ministry with prayer and finances over the years.

Finally, thanks to the Republican Women's Club of Chapel Hill, NC whose voracious appetite for truth inspires me. Thanks, Cheri and Pamela and Rosemarie and all the rest of the group.

Simple Islam

Table of Contents

Overview

Introduction

Part I - Consider the Facts

Part II - Contrast the Faith

Overview

The grace of God is more important than all the facts and history in this little book. Especially for Muslims, the love of Yehovah God must come through in our words and actions. Christ died for them as much as anyone on earth, so we emphasize His love and sacrifice. Yet, we will also expose the truth behind the system of Islam that enslaves its followers. And I hope to make it simple. Many Muslim individuals are finding forgiveness and love in Jesus. There are even many reports of Jesus appearing to them directly in dreams and visions. I rejoice with every report.

Islam is not hard to understand. It is made too complex by the very ones who try to explain it. My purpose is to reveal Islam in simplicity. This is not written for theologians or academics, yet it conforms to accurate historical and Biblical standards. Each point is supported by ample evidence, ensuring a "true report".

My goal with this little book is that you will find it a handy guide to keep around to refresh your own knowledge of Islam, and also to equip your sharing of simple, yet accurate, information with your friends.

The most important point of this entire book is that Jesus died for Muslims. God loves Muslims along with the whole world. Muslims are people. Islam is the religious/political system that enslaves them. We love the Muslim people, but reject Islam. From its inception it has had a violent and bloody history. It started with Muhammad's murders of many. Then, when he died, there began a series of bloody battles that produced the first major split of Islam into the two largest "denominations" of Sunni and Shia. History provides context for today's advance of Islam.

While we are at war with the system of Islam, we can love Muslims to life in Jesus. My hope is that this book will clarify this path. The Bible is clear that Yehovah will judge the wicked, but His heart is to show mercy to all who turn (repent) from their wickedness.

> *The Lord isn't really being slow about his promise, as some people think. No, he is being patient for your sake. He does not want anyone to be destroyed, but wants everyone to repent.* 2 Peter 3:9 NLT

My trek to make it simple began several years ago, when my brother Ken asked me to write a book about Islam. I have already written several books about Israel and the God of Israel. But I found it difficult writing about Islam. I gathered enough reference material to write a series of Islam books and was completely dissatisfied with my approach. Then I believe the Holy Spirit nudged me to start with a simple little bookmark, which I called a "Quick Guide to Islam". I mailed it to my brother and told him my "book" was in the mail. Even though the bookmark has been a great help to many, Ken continued to ask me for more. Now, the Holy Spirit has released me to offer this simple view of Islam.

First, I will present the basic message of the book mark, and then proceed to consider the factual history of Islam. We will continue with the non-negotiable differences between Islam according to the Quran, and the Biblical record. After we have an idea of the competing messages, we conclude by comparing the fruit of Islam to the fruit of Biblical faith.

The final result is this small book which gives more information than the bookmark, but I hope it keeps with the idea the Lord gave me, to keep it simple. My prayer is that many more will find it useful.

Introduction

Quick Guide to Islam

The idea for a bookmark was to mention the fewest possible summary points about Islam. It is the irreducible minimum you need to know about Islam a "Quick Guide to Islam". The content of that bookmark is included here. I truly believe it is all you need to know about Islam. I have expanded it to this little book to provide background information confirming these facts.

1. We do not all worship the same God.

2. Islam's god is not a father.

3. Islam's god has no son.

4. Islam's god is not Yehovah, the God of Abraham, Isaac and Jacob.

Contrast these facts with the following verses.

Who has ascended into heaven, or descended? Who has gathered the wind in His fists? Who has bound the waters in a garment? Who has established all the ends of the earth? **What is His name, and what is His Son's name,** *if you know?* (Proverbs 30:4)

The god of the Quran commands <u>your son</u> to die for him. The Living God of the Bible sent <u>His Son</u> to die for you.

Who is a liar but he who denies that Jesus is the Christ? He is antichrist who denies the Father and the Son. (1 John 2:22)

Don't Confuse Me with the Facts

Islam does not exist in a vacuum. It did not "just fall off the turnip truck" as the saying goes. There is a clear historical record of the birth of Islam. We **know** where it came from. Islam has an historical relationship with Jews and Christians, and their contrasting doctrines of faith and practice. We **know** the differences in their beliefs and their treatment of Bible believers. Even the Quran makes the distinction, calling Jews and Christians "People of the Book". There is a clear record of the practice of Islam for nearly 1,400 years. We **know** what follows the "wave" of Islamic conquest and migration. We will look at the facts of history in Part I: Consider the Facts.

It Matters What You Believe

If a pagan nation worships cows and rats, as gods, it should not be a surprise that they battle perennial famines, because they won't eat the cows for food or kill the rats that eat their grain. There are stark differences between Islam and the Bible. These are not subtle shades of interpretation, but totally opposite belief systems that are completely incompatible. And it really does matter. It is life and death. This applies not only to eternal life, but it even plays out in this life. We study these contradictory doctrines in Part II: Contrast the Faiths.

By Their Fruits You Will Know Them

What results from following Islam? ...in the personal life of a Muslim? ...in the cultural context of their people and nations? ...and what effect does Islam have on the rest of the geo-political world? In other words, what on earth is happening with the rise of Islam?

Jesus clearly warned His followers:

> *Beware of false prophets, who come to you in sheep's clothing, but inwardly they are ravenous wolves. You will know them by their fruits. Do men gather grapes from thornbushes or figs from thistles? Even so, every good tree bears good fruit, but a bad tree bears bad fruit. A good tree cannot bear bad fruit, nor can a bad tree bear good fruit. Every tree that does not bear good fruit is cut down and thrown into the fire. Therefore by their fruits you will know them.* Matthew 7:15-20

We will examine the fruits of Islam on three levels in Part III: Compare the Fruits.

What Should This Man Do?

What can be done, indeed? We should sound the alarm to awaken folks to the sinister purposes of Islam. But it is not hopeless. Is there hope for the world to avoid total domination by Islam's vision of world conquest? The answer is a resounding "Yes!" There is a victorious Plan of the Living God Yehovah. Millions of Muslims are crying out from the bondage of their heritage and turning to the God of the Bible and Yeshua ben Yehovah; they are finding Jesus, the Son of God.

15

They are discovering that they have been lied to; that the jesus (Isa) of the Quran is not the same person described in the Bible. Jesus is even appearing to Muslims supernaturally in dreams and visions, <u>calling them out of Islam</u> to living faith in the Messiah of Israel. Far from being against Muslims, I am totally for them. The famous John 3:16 verse explicitly declares that God the Father, sent His Son to die for all of us because <u>He loves the whole world</u>. We must love Muslims into the Kingdom of God. What a contrast to the god of Islam who <u>does not love infidels</u>! (Sura 2:190) **Simple Islam** concludes in Part Four, with **action items** to move us out of our lethargy and into passionate participation with God's great Plan of Redemption.

Clarifications:

1. **The name of the god of Islam** - You will notice that I have consistently miss-spelled the name of the god of Islam. This is intentional. My preference is to use this spelling "A-la" in place of the actual spelling of the name "Allah", except in direct quotes from other sources. I generally try to abide by the Biblical prohibition, given in at least four Scripture references where we are instructed to <u>not say the names of other gods</u>. These verses are explained in the conclusion of this book in Part IV - Action Items.

2. **Yehovah, God of Israel** - Also, notice that I use the Hebrew personal name for God, which is Yehovah (other acceptable pronunciations: Jehovah or Yahweh). It occurs 6,828 times in

the Hebrew text of the Old Testament, but is virtually unknown because the English translators substituted "LORD" (in all caps). It is now more important than ever that we use His name with the rise of the false god of Islam. I have explained this in my earlier books.

"I appeared to Abraham, to Isaac, and to Jacob, as God Almighty, but by My name Yehovah I was not known to them." Exodus 6:3

3. **Why Simple Islam?** - Finally, I chose the title **Simple Islam** because the revelation of Jesus comes from the Holy Spirit, who teaches us all we need to know about Islam in simplicity. If we get into the weeds of details about Islam, it gets complicated. Any study of "comparative religions" becomes very complex. Our starting point is the Bible itself. From the Biblical worldview, "other gods" is a simple concept.

*But I fear, lest somehow, as the serpent deceived Eve by his craftiness, so your minds may be corrupted from the **simplicity** that is in Christ. For if he who comes preaches another Jesus whom we have not preached, or if you receive a different spirit which you have not received, or a different gospel...* 2 Corinthians 11:3-4a

YEHOVAH IS FAITHFUL!

Part One: Consider the Facts

Chapter 1 - Voices from the Desert

Islam was founded by a man named Muhammad in the 7the Century AD, over 600 years after Jesus and the New Testament. He was born in 570 and died in 632 AD. He spoke of his visions and revelations during the last 23 years of his life. These were compiled into one book called the Quran after his death by the third Caliph in 650 AD. Muhammad used some Bible references, changing them freely to his own liking. He also claimed Divine inspiration for new revelations that he claimed he received from an angel named Gabriel. These differ sharply from the Biblical texts. He was a polytheist, worshipping many pagan gods of the Arabian Desert. He chose one of those many gods, a moon god named A-la to be his only god, thus he became a "monotheist". His verbal recitations became the basis for Quran and other writings in collections called the Sunnah and Hadith. These are the sources of Sharia Law, the governing authority for all faithful Muslims. (I intentionally misspell the god of Islam's name because the Bible instructs us not to say the name of pagan gods. (See Chapter 11)

Muhammad was not sinless. He never performed a single miracle. He did not die for anyone. No personal relationship with him is possible: he is dead.

Pagans who lived in Saudi Arabia before Muhammad was born worshiped toward Mecca because Mecca is where their idols were located. Because this pagan worship centered on Mecca was so widespread, a rapid acceptance of Muhammad's new religion was possible. Thus, Islam is a previously heathen religion modified into a monotheistic form by discarding all the other pagan gods except for Allah ... Archaeological and linguistic work done since the latter part of the 19th century has discovered overwhelming evidence that Muhammad constructed his religion and the Quran from pre- existing material in Arabian culture. (Notes and References on Islam by Chuck Missler http://www.ldolphin.org/missler.html)

Submission: Voluntary or Imposed?

Islam is the name of the religion and political system. People who follow Islam are called Muslims. Islam is translated "submission", which is a source of confusion for Christians and Jews. It is deceptive because we believe in voluntary submission, but Islam imposes submission at the point of the sword. Islamic conquerors only give three options to the vanquished:

1. Convert/submit to become a Muslim.
2. Submit to slavery or second-class (dhimmi) citizenship.
3. Die (traditionally by be-heading, among other ways).

We will say more about this in Chapter 2 as we discuss the contrasting faiths. Islam is often called "one of the world's three great monotheistic faiths."

Islam was not practiced before the 7th Century AD, in spite of the claims of modern Muslims. They claim Abraham, Moses and Jesus were all Muslims. This claim is a major contradiction of the Bible, of course. However, the demonic spirit behind Islam did exist during Old Testament times in the form of pagan moon worshipers as is evidenced in Judges 8.

> So Zebah and Zalmunna said, "Rise yourself, and kill us; for as a man is, so is his strength." So Gideon arose and killed Zebah and Zalmunna, and took the **crescent ornaments** that were on their camels' necks. Judges 8:21

The Hebrew root word for **crescent ornaments** is *"saharon"* and means: *moon, crescent a) as ornament*

The real problem of moon worshipers is that they worship created things rather than the Creator!

> For since the creation of the world His invisible attributes are clearly seen, being understood by the things that are made, even His eternal power and Godhead, so that they are without excuse, because, although they knew God, they did not glorify Him as God, nor were thankful, but became futile in their thoughts, and their foolish hearts were darkened. Professing to be wise, they became fools, and changed the glory of the incorruptible God into an image made

21

like corruptible man—and birds and four-footed animals and creeping things.

Therefore God also gave them up to uncleanness, in the lusts of their hearts, to dishonor their bodies among themselves, who exchanged the truth of God for the lie, and **worshiped and served the creature rather than the Creator,** *who is blessed forever.* Amen. Romans 1:20-25

Islam Divides the World

Islam only sees two opposing forces in the whole world:

1. Dar Al Islam: the domain of the faithful (to Islam)
2. Dar Al Harb: <u>those with whom they are at war until Judgment Day</u>. This second group includes not only Jews, but Christians, Hindus, Buddhists and every other religion, agnostics, atheists, and secularists. It even includes apostate (unfaithful) Muslims.

Now keep in mind that this world-view is true Islam. Not all Muslims are committed, but it is the fundamental position of the Quran. The numbers are not important. A minority holding this radical adherence have been successful in taking over territory because of their political system of Sharia, and the religious fervor of demonically empowered total passion. This is how a minority in number is able to dominate the majority.

It should be noted here that Islam itself has bitter divisions that war against each other. The main division is between

Sunni Arabs and Shia Iranians. Both however share the above worldview and both practice Sharia.

Muhammad's Wives

The Quraysh tribe (Muhammad's tribe) was previously devoted to Allah, the moon god. Muhammad's father was Abd-Allah. His Uncle, Obied-Allah. His mother, Aminah, was known to have been involved in the occult.

(The Quran's chapters are called Suras. Sura 4:3 forbids more than 4 wives; Muhammad, however had 16 official wives and 6 others as well.)

1. Khadija, 2. Sawda, 3. Aesah (8 or 9 years old), 4. Omm Salama, 5. Hafsa, 6. Zaynab (originally Jahsh's, Muhammad's adopted son's wife.) 7. Jowayriya, 8. Omm Habiba, 9. Safiya, 10. Maymuna (of Hareth) 11. Fatima, 12. Hend, 13. Asma (of Saba), 14. Zaynab (of Khozayma), 15. Habla 16. Asma (of Noman).

Other wives:

17. Mary (the Coptic Christian; chose to remain a slave rather than convert.) 18. Rayhana , 19. Omm Shank, 20. Maymuna , 21. Zaynab (a 3rd), 22. Khawla

(Notes and References on Islam by Chuck Missler http://www.ldolphin.org/missler.html)

The world's fastest growing religion, Islam is on a collision course with destiny.

"In 1984, Leon Uris explained that his purpose in writing The Haj, a novel, was to warn the West 'that we have an enraged bull of a billion people on our planet, and tilted the wrong way they could open the second road to Armageddon.'" Daniel Pipes, National Review 11-19-90

Another famous event in 1989 involves the author Salmon Rushdie, who was forced into permanent hiding because of death threats. His novel, <u>Satanic Verses</u>, was supposedly blasphemous against Islam. What a curious form of book review: if you don't like the book, kill the author. What kind of culture nurtures this kind of violent environment? These threats were not from some fringe fanatic terrorist, but from the spiritual head of fundamentalist Islam, the ruler of Iran, a rising nation of great power in the Islamic world. With the diminished influence of Iraq after the Eight Year War with Iran (which claimed one million lives), and the Gulf War humiliation and defeat of Saddam Hussein of Iraq by the West, Iran resumed its place as the leader of the militant masses of Shia Islam along with Sunni Turkey and Egypt. Dictators and Ayatollahs may rise and fall, and yet, the murderous spirit lives on in the next leader. Who are these Islamists and where do they get the spirit that motivates them? Many Muslims who are born into this slavish system want to get out of the bondage and are turning to the liberty of Jesus, the Son of Yehovah God.

YEHOVAH IS FAITHFUL!

Chapter Two - Early Roots of Islam

Islam is the name of the religion and its believers are known as Muslims. The common definition of the Arabic word "Islam" is submission. The idea of submission in their culture comes from the Quran, the Islamic holy book. This submission is in direct contrast to the Christian and Jewish submission which presupposes that the submission is voluntary. Islam demands submission in the sense of domination and control. Imposed submission is the fundamental non-negotiable lowest common denominator of Islam.

The majority of secular historians and sociologists consider Islam to be one of the world's "three great monotheistic religions". In one sense this is true, because they claim no god but A-la. But it gets confusing when the implication is given that A-la is the same "one" God that is worshipped by Jews and Christians. This error is repeated every day in today's media by inserting the word "God" in quotes from Arabic Muslim leaders like Palestinian Leader Mahmoud Abbas or President Muhammad Morsi of Egypt. When they are speaking in Arabic they are saying A-la, not God. If the media would use the word A-la, the viewer would get an entirely different sense of what is actually being said in the quotation. They would get it, that the god of Islam is a different god with a different name. His name is not the generic word "god", but a specific historical name of a desert moon god of Saudi Arabia.

Muhammad founded the formal religion between 613 and 624 A.D. This culminated in 625 with the conquering of Mecca and the beginning of his widespread acceptance as more than another desert warrior. I would like to follow the trail back further, however, because the spirit of Islam preceded the codification of the religion.

A-la is, in fact, one of the Baals or Baal gods that were prominent deities of pagans all through the Old Testament. That list includes the Canaanites, the Amalekites, the Middianites, and the Babylonians. The primary gods of Babylon, Marduke and Ishtar seemed to keep popping up in every pagan society under different names, but traceable back to Babylon. In Canaan they were known as Molech and Astarte, and together with Chomesh, Dagon, and other demonic "deities" were known as the Baals. I believe that the full name of Allah is Ba-Allah or Baallah. There is an amazing clue in the story of Gideon (circa 1200 B.C.) after he had seen the victory over the Middianites; as the 120,000-man army turned on one another with the resulting death of 105,000. The two kings of Midian escaped with 15,000 troops, but were soon overtaken by Gideon and routed with the capture of the two kings. The death of the two kings holds the fascinating clue as recorded in Judges 8:21

> "So Zebah and Zalmunna said, "Rise yourself, and kill us; for as a man is, so is his strength." So Gideon arose and killed Zebah and Zalmunna, and took the crescent ornaments that were on their camels' necks."

It was not enough to simply kill them, but as I wrote in Chapter One, he took the "crescent ornaments" from the necks of their camels! Could this indicate a connection between their Baal worship and Islam? The crescent is the primary symbol of Islam.

It is generally recognized by most historians that the Arab people descended from Ishmael. His name is as common among Moslems as Bill or Bob is to Americans, although the spelling varies (such as Ismail).

> *Historians say the original Arabs were a semi-nomadic, Semitic-speaking tribal people who dwelled in the northern section of the Arabian Peninsula, southeast of the Holy land. The Bible records that the peoples who roamed the northern Arabian Desert area were largely the descendants of Abraham's firstborn son, Ishmael, and Isaac's son Esau, also known as Edom. God promised Abraham that He would make Ishmael a great nation, although He made clear that He would establish His covenant with Isaac (Gen. 17:20-21). The God of Israel also foretold that there would be enmity between the descendants of Isaac's twin sons, Jacob and Esau (Gen.25:23). Esau's children began to fulfill that prophecy when they refused passage to the children of Israel who were on their way from Egypt to the Promised Land.* David Dolan, Holy War for the Promised Land (Nashville: Thomas Nelson Publishers, 1991) p.38-39

The Spirit of Islam

Spiritual demonic forces are infusing Islam today. These are pure paganism and occultism. There is no middle ground, no compromise with this bloodthirsty spirit; the bottom line is violent conquest. The fact that they say what we want to hear is actually a doctrine of lying called taqiyya. They are instructed that lying is a righteous way to achieve a desired effect for the advance of Islam and they will be rewarded for their "successful" lie. If you understand that this is true, it is a lot easier to understand their love of the Western media. They just tell us what we want to hear while going about their secretive purposes. An example of this in the 1990's was when Yassar Arafat "renounced terrorism" because the U.S President Bill Clinton required it as a precondition of initiating direct dialogue with us. Within a short time he was proven to be behind several new acts of terrorism. We were very indignant, because we did not understand Islam. But, he did not decide to stop terrorism; he simply agreed to "say" he would stop. To him it was not even a conflict of logic! Will our State Department ever learn this lesson? This "lying spirit" is just the tip of the iceberg. We are repeating the same error today with Iran and President Obama.

The major demonic principality behind Islam is Molech, (or Marduk) the Babylonian and Canaanite Baal god. In our search for biblical answers concerning Israel's right to the Land, it is good to know why the previous (Canaanite) inhabitants were dispossessed of their right. You may recall it was the worship of this deity and its pagan relatives that was the original reason for the Canaanites being kicked out of the Holy Land, especially child sacrifice "pass through the fire" as stated:

> *When you come into the land which Yehovah your God is giving you, you shall not learn to follow the*

*abominations of those nations. **There shall not be found among you anyone who makes his son or his daughter <u>pass through the fire</u>,** or one who practices witchcraft, or a soothsayer, or one who interprets omens, or a sorcerer, or one who conjures spells, or a medium, or a spiritist, or one who calls up the dead. For all who do these things are an abomination to Yehovah, and **because of these abominations Yehovah your God drives them out from before you.*** Deuteronomy 18:9-12

YEHOVAH IS FAITHFUL!

Chapter Three – Who is Molech?

Who was this pagan god who demanded child sacrifice (passing through the fire)?

A wide variety of practices is cited. An "enchanter" is a whisperer or snake charmer; a witch, one who uses charms or spells; a wizard, one who claimed to know the secrets of the other world; a necromancer, one who inquires of the dead, and so on. But the key evil is Molech worship. The word Moloch (or Melech, Melek, or Malik), meaning king, is a misvocalization of the name of a pagan, the consonants of king being retained and the vowels of shame used. Human sacrifice was made to this god, who is identified as the god of Ammon in I Kings 11:7,33." "Molech is "the king" or "kingship." The name of Moloch is also given as Milcom (I Kings 6:5, 33) and Malcam (Jer. 49:1, 3 RV; Zeph. 1:5). Moloch was an aspect of Baal (Jer. 32:35), Baal meaning lord. Under the name of Melcarth, king of Tyre, Baal was worshipped with human sacrifices at Tyre.

Since Moloch represented kinship and power, sacrifices to Moloch represented the purchase, at the very least, of immunity or insurance and protection, and, at its highest claim, of power. The "higher" sacrifices in paganism, and especially Baal worship, were sacrifices of humanity, i.e., self-mutilations, notably castration, the sacrifice of children or of posterity, and the like.

The priest became identified with the god to the degree that he "departed" from humanity by his castration, his separation from normal human relationships, and his abnormalities. The king became identified with the god to the degree that he manifested absolute power. The sacrifice of children was the supreme sacrifice to Moloch. Rousas John Rushdoony, The Institutes of Biblical Law (The Presbyterian and Reformed Publishing Company, 1973) pp.32-33

What kind of a god was Moloch? He was the god of the sacrifice of newborn babies. This was the central act of his worship; the firstborn of every woman's body had to be sacrificed to Moloch. According to one tradition, there was an opening at the back of the brazen idol, and after a fire was made within it, each parent had to come and with his own hands place his firstborn child in the white-hot, out-stretched hands of Molech. According to this tradition, the parent was not allowed to show emotion, and drums were beaten so that the baby's cries could not be heard as the baby died in the hands of Molech. Francis Schaeffer, The Church Before The Watching World, pp. 145-146

Here is a specific look at the connections of the occult to Islam.

Even before Islam was formed by Muhammad, the Arabian tribes had a custom of traveling to Mecca and worshipping a strange cube of black rock called the 'ka'abba,' which some scholars believe to be a meteorite. Later, when Judean folklore began to take hold among the nomads, some old-wives stories began circulating among the primitive Arab tribes. They were told that this rock 'had been raised by Adam, destroyed by the flood, and rebuilt by Abraham with the help of his son Ishmael, the father of all Arabs.' These fables were incorporated into Islam. Today this stone may be found in the corner of the central mosque in Mecca. According to another Quranic legend, it fell from paradise during the reconstruction of the Temple. The god of this stone in the old pagan Ka'abba religion was called Allah. A spirit of that same name spoke to the founder of Islam in visions, and he adopted the name for his god.

Muhammad invaded and conquered Mecca. The superstitious natives believed that such a victory was divinely inspired, and duly gave him their allegiance. There Muhammad denounced the plurality of gods, and proclaimed the sole deity of Allah. All human beings, he said, must be (in literal translation) the 'slaves of Allah,' which is also the meaning of the term 'Islam.' A 'Moslem' is 'one who submits.' Further, the Islamic term for 'peace' ('salaam') also means 'to submit.' Muhammad's view of world peace was a world totally dominated and submissive to the rule of Islam. Today, Islamic radicals still believe in world conquest - ruled by Islamic dictatorships governed by the sharia, Islam's barbaric Cannon law. --- As for the pagan customs of his people, he incorporated many of them into his religion. Indeed, the concepts of honorable blood-shedding, shame and the sacred vendetta, or blood-feud, were made holy. Muhammad - the offspring of a violent, savage heritage - could not understand the vital importance of the concept of peace and coexistence that underlines both Christianity and Judaism. True to his legacy he conceived a religion of warfare and struggle, in which the war was holy (jihad) and tolerance baneful, and in which the very meaning of the word 'peace' came to mean not cooperation and the acceptance of others, but precisely the opposite - the total destruction (or submission) of the enemy. Even today, Islamic terrorists use the word 'peace' when communicating with the West. However, 'peace' has a very different meaning to a religious Moslem. Professor Peter A. Michas, <u>What Is Islam</u>? (Poway, CA: The Christian Mid-East Conference, 1991).

Now that we have caught a glimpse of the violent spirit of Molech that is behind Islam, what do they actually believe?

YEHOVAH IS FAITHFUL!

Part II: Contrast the Faiths

Chapter Four – Who is the False Prophet?

The desert god A-la is a different god than the God of Israel, the God of Abraham, Isaac and Jacob. I believe, in fact that Islam is a counterfeit religion of Judaism and Christianity. We will now examine facts to confirm that point. Modern Islam has to answer for and defend its own book, the Quran. In this section we will look at some of the claims of the Quran in the light of the Bible. First, let us hear what Derek Prince, a widely esteemed international Bible teacher, taught on the subject.

> *The strongest spiritual force that opposes God's purposes and God's people in the Middle East today is Islam, the Muhammadan religion. Yet, Muhammad, the founder of Islam, was a false prophet. As such, his words and the movement he brought into being will ultimately be brought to naught. Some may be inclined to challenge the statement that Muhammad was a false prophet. To this I would offer one brief and simple response: If Jesus was a true prophet, then Muhammad was a false prophet. Following are a few of the main points in which the teaching of Muhammad contradicts that of Jesus.*
>
> *1. Jesus declared that He was the Son of God. Islam totally rejects the idea that God can have a son,*

dismissing it as blasphemy. Islam further rejects the concept of one God revealed in three Persons.

2. Historically, the Christian faith has centered around the crucifixion and resurrection of Jesus, Islam denies that Jesus ever actually died on the cross, or that He was resurrected.

3. Jesus claimed He had come to fulfill the Law and the prophets (Matt. 5:17). Islam claims that it alone is the true fulfillment and completion of the revelation contained in the Old and New Testaments.

4. Jesus promised His followers that He would send them 'another Comforter' (John 14:15-17, 26 KJV). The Christian Church has always taught that this promise was fulfilled by the coming of the Holy Spirit on the Day of Pentecost. Islam claims that Muhammad was the Comforter promised by Jesus.

5. The Old Testament, which Jesus accepted as authoritative, states clearly that Abraham offered his son Isaac on the altar on Mount Moriah (Gen. 22:9-12). Islam claims that Ishmael was the son whom Abraham offered.

The direct opposition of the teaching of Muhammad to that of Jesus is mirrored at large in the contemporary world situation, and particularly in the Middle East. There is a single, spiritual force that unites the nations of the Middle East in fierce, unyielding opposition to the outworking of God's purposes for Israel: it is Islam.

Derek Prince, The Last Word On The Middle East (Chosen Books 1982), pp. 68-69.

Muslims do not believe in original sin, that all are naturally sinful. Therefore, they see no need of a Savior. We know that Adam fell and anyone born after Adam does not have the Spirit of God in them until they are "born again" in Jesus, the Divine Son of God. This opens the heart of a Muslim to Yehovah God, Jesus and the Holy Spirit. The fact that they deny Jesus' death; means they have no basis for forgiveness:

> And according to the law almost all things are purified with blood, and without [shedding of blood] there is no remission. Hebrews 9:22

By denying the blood sacrifice of Jesus (once, and for all who believe); they must live enslaved by their sins. By insisting that their god is indivisible, they deny the Trinity.

Look at these quotes from the Quran extracted by David Dolan.

> "The Islamic holy book urges all Muslims to 'make war' on the unbelievers 'until idolatry is no more and Allah's religion reigns supreme' (Sura 8:39). The reward for dying in a jihad struggle is instantaneous entrance into paradise, which the Quran makes clear is a place of great sensual pleasure. Modern Muslim apologists maintain that jihad does not necessarily mean actual fighting. Jihad is also waged by nonviolent struggle through education, propaganda and economic boycott. But it is abundantly clear from the Quran (and from the

37

Hadith, the codified Islamic oral tradition of Muhammad's actions and sayings) that the primary meaning of jihad is actual fighting - 'holy war.' That is why Islam has long been known as the religion of the sword." --- "Conversion to Islam was a very simple matter, as it is today. One had only to recite three times the <u>Shahada</u>, the <u>Islamic Affirmation of Faith</u>: 'There is no God but Allah, and Muhammad is the Prophet of Allah.'"

According to the Quran, Jesus is not the Son of God, but 'the son of Mary,' since God could not have a son. Those who declare that Jesus is God are 'unbelievers' who will be 'forbidden entrance into Paradise, and shall be cast into the fire of hell,' for 'the Messiah, the son of Mary, was no more than an apostle' (Sura 5:73-75). The Quran's version of the birth of Jesus is very different from the Gospel accounts. In Sura Mary (Sura means 'revelation'), the Holy Spirit is sent to Mary in the form of a full-grown man who tells the frightened Jewish maiden that he has 'come to give you a holy son' (15-20). The Quranic account then reveals that Jesus came into the world while Mary rested under a palm tree somewhere in 'the east.' Suddenly a voice comes 'from below' her, apparently the newborn baby Jesus, who tells Mary to shake the tree and eat of its fruit (24-27). Later the infant surprises Mary's relatives by speaking from his cradle, saying, 'I am the servant of Allah,' and describing his mission on earth. The Quran then reveals that 'this is the whole truth, which they (apparently the Christians and Jews) are unwilling to accept,' adding that 'Allah forbid that He Himself should beget a son!' (29-36)." ---"'Say: Praise be to Allah who has never begotten a son, who has no partner in His kingdom. (Sura 17:111). David Dolan, <u>Holy War for the Promised Land</u> (Nashville: Thomas Nelson Publishers, 1991) pp. 46,42-43

Those last two quotes from the Quran are among dozens of like quotes, denying the Sonship of Jesus, that are written in two-foot-high Arabic letters around the inside of the Dome of the Rock, the Muslim shrine on the Temple Mount in Jerusalem. Perhaps you now have a better understanding of the real reasons for the conflicts in the Middle East.

Jesus Died

Islam denies that Jesus died; some even suggesting it was Judas on the cross. This is a critical error and denial of the Bible. The Messiah's death as the Lamb of God is non-negotiable. Jesus became the sinless sacrificial Lamb who paid for our sin with His own blood. If He did not die, then we are still in our sin and there is no forgiveness. The very concept of forgiveness is foreign to the Quran. No wonder Muslims have a difficult time accepting that their sins can be washed away and forgiven by the grace of Yehovah God. This concept is in both the Old and New Testaments. Pray that Muslims will learn of His forgiveness.

*(The following is an excerpt from my book, **Generation LIFE** Chapter 1 – Jesus is Alive, published 2012.)*

Do you believe in Him, I mean, do you really believe Him? Do you follow Him? Do you have a deep desire in your innermost being to be like Him? I want to know all I can know about Jesus. Getting to know Him personally is really possible. Do you know Him?

Do you believe He really died? Or do you think He just sort of passed out and then woke up a little later? If Jesus didn't die, we are still in our sin. Guilty! I want to talk about His resurrection LIFE, but first we need to get this. Jesus really died. He was dead. He was so dead that He Himself could not come back to life. We need to understand this. It was not a charade. When He gave up His last breath, He was utterly dependent on the faithful true Promise of His Father to live again. That is why this chapter is named: Jesus is Alive. Of course He was eternally alive and existed with the Father before Creation, and He is alive now. But between, for three days, He was dead.

You may think it strange to begin a book about life with a dead Jesus. But, if you don't know that He died and why He died, you are missing the best part. Yes, it is the resurrection, but it is meaningless if He did not die. Jesus died, and on the third day, rose again. Hallelujah! I really want to talk about His life. But we must understand His death to appreciate the all-encompassing glory of the Gospel of the Kingdom of God. Jesus did not then, nor does He now possess some super power called "resurrection power". If it were up to Him, He would still be dead. As we will soon see, Jesus is LIFE, He is resurrection LIFE. It is His own personal experience of redemption from death. Here is a verse to confirm how He was raised back to life.

> But if **the Spirit of Him who raised Jesus from the dead** dwells in you, <u>He who raised Christ from the dead</u> will also give life to your mortal bodies through His Spirit who dwells in you Romans 8:11.

So Jesus was dead and was resurrected by the Holy Spirit of God. We know that Jesus lived by the Spirit and was raised by the Spirit. Therefore, through His ultimate trust in Yehovah, the Father, He qualified to die for all who believe in His finished work. I honestly believe in Him, do you?

He is no longer in the grave, He arose from the dead. Jesus is alive!

> Therefore I will divide Him a portion with the great, And He shall divide the spoil with the strong, Because He poured out His soul unto death, And He was numbered with the transgressors, And He bore the sin of many, And made intercession for the transgressors. Isaiah 53:12

YEHOVAH IS FAITHFUL!

Chapter Five – The Intention of Islam

Well, it should be plain by now. Islam intends to dominate the entire world. Their theology allows for nothing else. This is tempered somewhat by the previously mentioned divisions within the religion such as Sunni/Shia and on smaller scale in Egypt between competing Islamist Sunni groups, the Muslim Brotherhood and the more extreme Salafis. Nevertheless, each group has the ultimate goal of dominating the world and form temporary confederacies toward a common goal such as attacking Israel. See Psalm 83.

> To this day, it is a cardinal tenet of Islam to divide the world into two irreconcilable camps, the dar al-Islam or 'house of Islam', which includes all countries where Islam currently prevails, and the dar al-harb or 'house of war', which includes everywhere else. The object of Islam and its promoters is to expand their power until all is within their realm. It is a global vision, similar to that used until recently by Communism, but more powerful because it is a religion, not a political ideology. Dr. Gayle Kesselman, About Islam (Kesselman Foundation).

The rule of Christians is only tolerated temporarily. The rule of Jews, especially in the "Arab Middle East", is intolerable. In either case Islam views the situation as temporary, only a matter of time.

> The late Iranian leader Ayatollah Khomeini taught that Satan created 'that cancerous tumor' Israel, with

Allah's approval, as a judgment on backslidden Muslim nations. When Muslims, especially decadent Western-inspired leaders, repent of their wicked ways, then Allah will destroy the 'infidel' state. To say the least, this view - widely believed by Palestinians - greatly impedes efforts to establish a lasting peace between the Muslim world and Israel.

Iranian leader Ayatollah Khameini, speaking on June 4, 1990 - the first anniversary of his predecessor Ayatollah Khomeini's death, vowed that Iran will not rest until Israel is destroyed. David Dolan, <u>Holy War for the Promised Land</u> (Nashville: Thomas Nelson Publishers, 1991) p. 213.

Obviously, the Middle East, and indeed the world, is on a collision course with destiny. The problem for Islam is that they clash with the world on both ends of the spectrum. As we have seen, they clash with the Bible and its followers. But they also have a major contradiction with the New Agers of the New World Order of humanism, because Islam's most adamant pillar of faith is "No god but A-la." This kind of intolerance would not be allowed in the "New Order" where any religion would be encouraged as long as it does not claim it is the only way to God. Religious intolerance would be outlawed because it limits "freedom of religion". Of course, this is a point that also conflicts with true Christianity because of Jesus' words:

Jesus said to him, I am the way, the truth, and the life. No one comes to the Father except through Me. John 14:6

At the present, Islam and one-worlders are working together, but I believe Islam will prevail between the two.

Today's Hamas Threat

Hamas in Gaza is an immediate threat. They are sponsored by Iran and are fundamentalists dedicated to the destruction of Israel. The meaning of their name in Hebrew is "violence." It is the exact word used in Genesis 6:13: *And God said to Noah, "The end of all flesh has come before Me, for the earth is filled with violence through them; and behold, I will destroy them with the earth.*

David Dolan has an interesting quote from the Hamas Covenant:

> *Article 6 says HAMAS is 'working to unfurl the banner of Allah over every inch of Palestine.' Article 8 endorses martyrdom in the name of the holy jihad: 'Allah is the ultimate objective of HAMAS, his messenger Muhammad its touchstone, the Quran its constitution, 'jihad' its path, and death for the sake of Allah its chief interest.' Article 13 states that --- 'There is no solution to the Palestinian problem except through 'jihad'.* David Dolan, Holy War for the Promised Land (Nashville: Thomas Nelson Publishers, 1991) pp. 172-173

What about the salvation of the Arabs? Is there any hope for them? Or are they so bound in Islam that they will never find Jesus?

The Palestinian Arabs are definitely victims - but not primarily of the Israelis. They are, in my opinion, mainly the victims of an often-violent religion based on a corruption of the Bible. While I have great love and respect for the Muslims as people made in the image of God, I cannot but grieve for them as prisoners of a religious system, based on the Quran and Hadith, which exalts warfare and almost mandates hatred, or at least scorn, of the Jews. David Dolan, <u>Holy War for the Promised Land</u> (Nashville: Thomas Nelson Publishers, 1991) pp. 209

Those who believe that the church replaced Israel and became God's second wife should understand that Islam believes it has replaced both Israel and the church! God has never had another bride and never will. There is only one groom and only one bride. All who believe in Jesus are part of the bride, whether it was ancient Jews looking ahead in faith, or believers who look back in history to Jesus' sacrifice in faith. Of course Muslims can be saved if they turn from A-la and accept the God of Abraham, Isaac and Jacob, accepting Jesus as the Son of God. Philippians 2 says every knee will bow and every tongue will confess the Lordship of Jesus, to the glory of God, the Father. This does not mean all will be saved. It does mean all will bow and acknowledge that Jesus is Lord. They will either do it as those who are saved, with great joy and giving of thanks, or with total despair and defeat as the conquered enemy of God. But there is one thing for sure, there will be former Muslims saved and rejoicing with the rest of us.

And they sang a new song, saying: "You are worthy to take the scroll, And to open its seals; For You were slain, And have redeemed us to God by Your blood Out of every tribe and tongue and people and nation. Revelation 5:9

Pray for the salvation of some from "every tribe," including all people in the awful grip of Islam, that God will have mercy and reveal Jesus to them, before it is too late. I show the way through Jesus in Part Four: Action Items.

YEHOVAH IS FAITHFUL!

Chapter Six - Another Jesus?

But I fear, lest somehow, as the serpent deceived Eve by his craftiness, so your minds may be corrupted from the simplicity that is in Christ. **For if he who comes preaches <u>another Jesus</u> whom we have not preached,** *or if you receive a different spirit which you have not received, or a different gospel...I*

For such are false apostles, deceitful workers, transforming themselves into apostles of Christ. And no wonder! For Satan himself transforms himself into an angel of light. Therefore it is no great thing if his ministers also transform themselves into ministers of righteousness, whose end will be according to their works. 2 Corinthians 11:3-4, 13-15

I marvel that you are turning away so soon from Him who called you in the grace of Christ, to a different gospel, which is not another; but there are some who trouble you and want to pervert the gospel of Christ. **But even if we, or an angel from heaven, preach any other gospel to you than what we have preached to you, let him be accursed.** *As we have said before, so now I say again,* **if anyone preaches any other gospel to you than what you have received, let him be accursed.** *Galatians 1:6-9*

The Apostle Paul could not have been clearer in his warning. There have been many "other gospels" down through the years, but Islam is perhaps the most dangerous. Paul even saw the possibility of someone claiming: "An angel told me!" This is exactly the claim of Muhammad.

If you still have any doubt that Islam is "another gospel", here are five more comparisons between the Jesus of the Bible and the Jesus of the Quran whose Arabic name is Isa. (The Quran quotes here are from the English translation on the Internet at this address: www.dar-us-salam.com/TheNobleQuran/index.html)

1. Bible: Jesus is the Divine Son of God

    Who has ascended into heaven, or descended? Who has gathered the wind in His fists? Who has bound the waters in a garment? Who has established all the ends of the earth? **What is His name, and what is His Son's name,** If you know? Proverbs 30:4

    And the Word became flesh and dwelt among us, and we beheld His glory, **the glory as of the only begotten of the Father,** full of grace and truth. John 1:14

    For God so loved the world that He gave His only begotten Son, that whoever believes in Him should not perish but have everlasting life. John 3:16

    Quran: Isa is not Divine or the son of God.

    being a slave of Allah, and having no share in Divinity. Verily! This is the true narrative [about the story of 'Iesa (Jesus)], and, La ilaha ill-Allah (none has the right to be worshipped but Allah, *the One and the Only True God, Who has neither a wife nor a son).* Sura 3:61-62

O people of the Scripture (Jews and Christians)! Do not exceed the limits in your religion, nor say of Allah aught but the truth. The Messiah 'Iesa (Jesus), son of Maryam (Mary), was (no more than) a Messenger of Allah and His Word, ("Be!" - and he was) which He bestowed on Maryam (Mary) and a spirit (Ruh) created by Him; so believe in Allah and His Messengers. Say not: "Three (trinity)!" Cease! (it is) better for you. For Allah is (the only) One Ilah (God), Glory be to Him (Far Exalted is He) above having a son. To Him belongs all that is in the heavens and all that is in the earth. And Allah is All-Sufficient as a Disposer of affairs. Sura 4:171

*And they say: "The Most Beneficent (Allah) has begotten a son (or offspring or children) [as the Jews say: 'Uzair (Ezra) is the son of Allah, and the Christians say that He has begotten a son ['Iesa (Christ)], and the pagan Arabs say that He has begotten daughters (angels, etc.)]." Indeed you have brought forth (said) a terrible evil thing. Whereby the heavens are almost torn, and the earth is split asunder, and the mountains fall in ruins, That they ascribe a son (or offspring or children) to the Most Beneficent (Allah). **But it is not suitable for***

51

*(the Majesty of) the Most Beneficent (Allah)
that He should beget a son (or offspring or
children).* Sura 19:88-92 (For greater detail on
this subject, I highly recommend this excellent
website, Jesus is not in the Quran, by my friend,
Dale Suggs: www.jesusisnotinthequran.org/new-
read-this-first/

2. Bible: Jesus is eternal, not created.

> *But you, Bethlehem Ephrathah, though you are
> little among the thousands of Judah, Yet out of
> you shall come forth to Me the One to be Ruler
> in Israel,* **Whose goings forth are from of old,
> From everlasting.** Micah 5:2
>
> *He has delivered us from the power of
> darkness and conveyed us into the kingdom of
> the Son of His love, in whom we have
> redemption through His blood, the forgiveness
> of sins. He is the image of the invisible God, the
> firstborn over all creation.* **For by Him all
> things were created that are in heaven and
> that are on earth, visible and invisible,
> whether thrones or dominions or
> principalities or powers. All things were
> created through Him and for Him. And He is
> before all things, and in Him all things consist.**
> Colossians 1:13-17

Quran: Isa was created.

> *Verily, the likeness of 'Iesa (Jesus) before Allah
> is the likeness of Adam.* **He created him from**

dust, then (He) said to him: "Be!" - and he was.
Sura 3:59

3. Bible: Jesus is the Lamb of God.

The next day John saw Jesus coming toward him, and said, "Behold! The Lamb of God who takes away the sin of the world!" John 1:29
And they sang a new song, saying: "You are worthy to take the scroll, And to open its seals; For You were slain, And have redeemed us to God by Your blood Out of every tribe and tongue and people and nation, Revelation 5:9
Saying with a loud voice: "Worthy is the Lamb who was slain To receive power and riches and wisdom, And strength and honor and glory and blessing!" Revelation 5:12

Quran: Isa did not die.

And because of their saying (in boast), "We killed Messiah 'Iesa (Jesus), son of Maryam (Mary), the Messenger of Allah," - **but they killed him not, nor crucified him, but the resemblance of 'Iesa (Jesus) was put over another man (and they killed that man),** *and those who differ therein are full of doubts. They have no (certain) knowledge, they follow nothing but conjecture.* **For surely; they killed him not.** *Sura 4:157*

4. Bible: Jesus is the name above every name.

Which He worked in Christ when He raised Him from the dead and seated Him at His right hand in the heavenly places, far above all principality and power and might and dominion, and every name that is named, not only in this age but also in that which is to come. Ephesians 1:20-21

Quran: Isa is no greater than other prophets.

Say (O Muslims), "We believe in Allah and that which has been sent down to us and that which has been sent down to Ibrahim (Abraham), Isma'il (Ishmael), Ishaque (Isaac), Ya'qub (Jacob), and to Al-Asbat [the twelve sons of Ya'qub (Jacob)], and that which has been given to Musa (Moses) and 'Iesa (Jesus), and that which has been given to the Prophets from their Lord. **We make no distinction between any of them,** *and to Him we have submitted (in Islam)."* Sura 2:136

5. Bible: Jesus is to be worshipped.

Therefore God also has highly exalted Him and given Him the name which is above every name, that at the name of Jesus every knee should bow, of those in heaven, and of those on earth, and of those under the earth, and [that] every tongue should confess that Jesus Christ is Lord, to the glory of God the Father. Philippians 2:9-11

Quran: Isa is not to be worshipped.

And (remember) when Allah will say (on the Day of Resurrection): "O 'Iesa (Jesus), son of Maryam (Mary)! Did you say unto men: 'Worship me and my mother as two gods besides Allah?' " He will say: "Glory be to You! It was not for me to say what I had no right (to say). Had I said such a thing, You would surely have known it. You know what is in my inner-self though I do not know what is in Yours, truly, You, only You, are the All-Knower of all that is hidden and unseen. Sura 5:116

YEHOVAH IS FAITHFUL!

Part III: Compare the Fruits

A review of Biblical fruit is a helpful introduction to this next section comparing the fruit of Islam. Galatians offers the best concise contrast of fruit in human nature. We either yield to sinful fleshly desires or we submit to the Holy Spirit.

> Now the works of the flesh are evident, which are: adultery, fornication, uncleanness, lewdness, idolatry, sorcery, hatred, contentions, jealousies, outbursts of wrath, selfish ambitions, dissensions, heresies, envy, murders, drunkenness, revelries, and the like; of which I tell you beforehand, just as I also told you in time past, that those who practice such things will not inherit the kingdom of God. But the fruit of the Spirit is love, joy, peace, longsuffering, kindness, goodness, faithfulness, gentleness, self-control. Against such there is no law. And those who are Christ's have crucified the flesh with its passions and desires. If we live in the Spirit, let us also walk in the Spirit. Galatians 5:19-25

It is tempting to just look at those two lists and rest my case, but let's take a look at history.

Chapter Seven – John of Damascus

We looked at the Biblical viewpoint of Islam in Part I, and we examined the different claims of Jesus and the Christian faith contrasted with Islam and the Quran in Part II. Now we look at historical evidence showing the effect that Islam has wherever it goes.

> For every tree is known by its own fruit. For men do not gather figs from thorns, nor do they gather grapes from a bramble bush. A good man out of the good treasure of his heart brings forth good; and an evil man out of the evil treasure of his heart brings forth evil. For out of the abundance of the heart his mouth speaks.
> Luke 6:45

Islam has been observed to produce evil fruit from its beginning. Several early Christian reports have been preserved from the time of Islam's founding by Muhammad in Arabia 1,400 years ago around 610 AD (600 years after Jesus). Here are quotations from three historical reports.

> ***Sophronius, Patriarch of Jerusalem (560-638)*** *was an Arab Christian who became the Patriarch of Jerusalem in 634 and remained so until his death four years later. It was during these years that the Muslim armies under Caliph Umar invaded and conquered Jerusalem. Several historical references attest to the fact that Sophronius identified the Muslim occupation of Jerusalem and the Temple Mount as the fulfillment of the "abomination that causes desolation" that is*

always associated with the coming of the antichrist. Sophronius laments the circumstances under which the church in Jerusalem found itself and refers to the Muslim occupiers as being followers of Satan: "Why are the troops of the Saracens attacking us? Why has there been so much destruction and plunder? Why are there incessant outpourings of human blood? Why are the birds of the sky devouring human bodies? Why have churches been pulled down? Why is the cross mocked? Why is Christ, who is the dispenser of all good things and the provider of this joyousness of ours, blasphemed by pagan mouths...the vengeful and God-hating Saracens, the abomination of desolation clearly foretold to us by the prophets, overrun the places which are not allowed to them, plunder cities, devastate fields, burn down villages, set on fire the holy churches, overturn the sacred monasteries...Moreover, they are raised up more and more against us and increase their blasphemy of Christ and the Church, and utter wicked blasphemies against God. Those God-fighters boast of prevailing over all, assiduously and unrestrainedly imitating their leader, who is the devil, and emulating his vanity because of which he has been expelled from heaven and been assigned to the gloomy shades."

Maximus the Confessor (580-662) was an important theologian and scholar of the early Church who helped defeat the Monothelite heresy, which claimed that Christ only possessed a divine and not a human will.

Maximus witnessed the rise and spread of the Islamic Empire in his day. He described the invading Muslims as "a people who... delight in human blood... whom God hates, though they think they are worshipping God." He also referred to the Muslim invasions as "announcing the advent of the Antichrist." And so we see that even at such an early period of Islam's growth, a clear association of Islam with the antichrist prophecies was being articulated.

John of Damascus (646-749) *is another very important figure in the early Church. He was born into a privileged Christian family in Syria, but later became a presbyter and a monk. His grandfather had been the administer of Damascus at the time the Muslims took it, and he was thoroughly familiar with Islam and thus, in his famous book,* <u>Against Heresies,</u> *he devotes a whole chapter to the discussion of Islam.*

And there is also up until now a strong and people-deceiving superstition among Ishmaelites, that is the forerunner of Antichrist. And this (superstition-Islam) is born from Ishmael, who was born from Hagar to Abraham, from which they are called Hagarenes and Ishmaelites. And they call them Saracens, (those empty of Sarah), because of what was said by Hagar to the angel: "Sarah has sent me away empty." So then, these were idolaters and reverenced the morning star and Aphrodite, who they indeed named Akbar in their own language, which means great. Therefore, until the time of Heraclius, they were plainly idolaters. From that

61

time and until now came up among them a false prophet called Muhammad, who, having encountered the Old and New Testament, as it seems, having conversed with an Arian monk, he put together his own heresy.

Even as early as 50 years after Islam was birthed, learned Christian leaders who were familiar with Islam were referring to it as a forerunner of the antichrist. The Muslim invasions heralded "the advent of the antichrist." Interestingly we see John of Damascus pointing to Islam as a Christian heresy connected to an Arian monk, and his connection to Aphrodite, the moon-goddess. This is proven archeologically by early Islamic coins. Walid Shoebat with Joel Richardson, God's War on Terror (Top Executive Media 2008) p.328

Early Islamic invasions conquered Jerusalem killing Christians and burning down churches with great bloodshed. We see the same pattern today after 1,400 years; in Egypt, Sudan, Pakistan, Indonesia and African nations such Nigeria. This persecution occurs in some degree in most of the 157 modern Islamic nations. From India to the Philippines, churches are being burned and Christians martyred in the name of the god of Islam. Such violence is only destined to increase with the weakness of the West, and the rise of Islam. This is creating a new boldness in radical jihadists worldwide.

In the 20th century, Islam grew in Africa both by birth and by conversion. The number of Muslims in Africa grew from 34.5 million in 1900 to 315 million in 2000, going from roughly 20% to 40% of the total population of Africa. However, in the same time period, the number of Christians also grew in Africa, from 8.7 million in 1900 to 346 million in 2000, surpassing both the total population as well as the growth rate of Islam on the continent. en.wikipedia.org/wiki/Spread_of_Islam

We are seeing a colossal clash of civilizations today, no matter how many Western leaders deny it. There is a great cosmic battle for the souls of men. Jesus has purchase us with His own blood and now we belong to Yehovah God. All who refuse the Son of God are slaves of Satan, no matter what religion or philosophy. It matters what you believe. But there are more examples down through the centuries.

YEHOVAH IS FAITHFUL!

Chapter Eight – What about the Crusades?

The best answer I have seen to the "Crusade" issue is from Gregory M. Davis:

> The obvious response to this question is, "Well, what about them?" Violence committed in the name of other religions is logically unconnected to the question of whether Islam is violent. But, by mentioning the Crusades, the hope of the Islamic apologist is to draw attention away from Islamic violence and paint religions in general as morally equivalent.
>
> In both the Western academia and media as well as in the Islamic world, the Crusades are viewed as wars of aggression fought by bloody-minded Christians against peaceful Muslims. While the Crusades were certainly bloody, they are more accurately understood as a belated Western response to centuries of jihad than as an unprovoked, unilateral attack. Muslim rule in the Holy Land began in the second half of the 7th century during the Arab wave of jihad with the conquests of Damascus and Jerusalem by the second "rightly-guided Caliph," Umar. After the initial bloody jihad, Christian and Jewish life there was tolerated within the strictures of the dhimma and the Muslim Arabs generally permitted Christians abroad to continue to make pilgrimage to their holy sites, a practice which proved lucrative for the Muslim state.

Following the very bloody capture of Jerusalem in 1099 by the Latin armies and the establishment of the Crusader States in Edessa, Antioch, and Jerusalem, the Muslim and Christian forces fought a see-saw series of wars, in which both parties were guilty of the usual gamut of wartime immorality. Over time, even with reinforcing Crusades waged from Europe, the Crusader States, strung out on precarious lines of communication, slowly succumbed to superior Muslim power. In 1271, the last Christian citadel, Antioch, fell to the Muslims. No longer having to divert forces to subdue the Christian beachhead on the Eastern Mediterranean, the Muslims regrouped for a 400-year-long jihad against Southern and Eastern Europe, which twice reached as far as Vienna before it was halted. In geostrategic terms, the Crusades can be viewed as an attempt by the West to forestall its own destruction at the hands of Islamic jihad by carrying the fight to the enemy. It worked for a while.

Significantly, while the West has for some time now lamented the Crusades as mistaken, there has never been any mention from any serious Islamic authority of regret for the centuries and centuries of jihad and dhimmitude perpetrated against other societies. But this is hardly surprising: while religious violence contradicts the fundamentals of Christianity, religious violence is written into Islam's DNA. Gregory M. Davis Islam 101 www.jihadwatch.org/islam-101.html

The point he made at the beginning is important, that Muslims will try to use this issue to deflect attention, and especially criticism, from their own far bloodier history. Moral equivalence is a great propaganda tool used effectively as a paper tiger by Islam. True Christians reject the excesses of war while Islam continues their same pattern.

What about moderate Muslims?

One other point should be made about the idea of "peaceful Muslims". Rather than debate about the percentages of moderate or radical Muslims, the question is: "Does it matter?" Recent history teaches us that the Nazi's were a small percentage of Germans, but they dominated and nearly destroyed Europe and the world. There are about 1.5 billion Muslims. If only 10 per cent were radical, that would be 150 million. Even if only one per cent were violent jihadists, it would mean 15 million potential suicide bombers!

Our desire is to see millions of Muslims come to Jesus, the Son of God, for salvation and deliverance. I explain how this can happen at the end of this book.

YEHOVAH IS FAITHFUL!

Chapter 9 - Who were the Barbary pirates?

Or: What Thomas Jefferson learned from the Muslim book of jihad

By Ted Sampley U.S. Veteran Dispatch January 2007

Democrat Keith Ellison is now officially the first Muslim United States congressman. True to his pledge, he placed his hand on the Quran, the Muslim book of jihad and pledged his allegiance to the United States during his ceremonial swearing-in.

Capitol Hill staff said Ellison's swearing-in photo opportunity drew more media than they had ever seen in the history of the U.S. House. Ellison represents the 5th Congressional District of Minnesota.

The Quran Ellison used was no ordinary book. It once belonged to Thomas Jefferson, third president of the United States and one of America's founding fathers. Ellison borrowed it from the Rare Book Section of the Library of Congress. It was one of the 6,500 Jefferson books archived in the library.

Ellison, who was born in Detroit and converted to Islam while in college, said he chose to use Jefferson's Quran because it showed that "a visionary like Jefferson" believed that wisdom could be gleaned from many sources.

There is no doubt Ellison was right about Jefferson believing wisdom could be "gleaned" from the Muslim Quran. At the time Jefferson owned the book, he needed to know everything possible about Muslims because he was about to advocate war against the Islamic "Barbary" states of Morocco, Algeria, Tunisia and Tripoli.

Ellison's use of Jefferson's Quran as a prop illuminates a subject once well-known in the history of the United States, but, which today, is mostly forgotten - the Muslim pirate slavers who over many centuries enslaved millions of Africans and tens of thousands of Christian Europeans and Americans in the Islamic "Barbary" states.

Over the course of 10 centuries, Muslim pirates cruised the African and Mediterranean coastline, pillaging villages and seizing slaves.

The taking of slaves in pre-dawn raids on unsuspecting coastal villages had a high casualty rate. It was typical of Muslim raiders to kill off as many of the "non-Muslim" older men and women as possible so the preferred "booty" of only young women and children could be collected.

Young non-Muslim women were targeted because of their value as concubines in Islamic markets. Islamic law provides for the sexual interests of Muslim men by allowing them to take as many as four wives at one time and to have as many concubines as their fortunes allow.

Boys, as young as 9 or 10 years old, were often mutilated to create eunuchs who would bring higher prices in the slave markets of the Middle East. Muslim slave traders created "eunuch stations" along major African slave routes so the necessary surgery could be performed. It was estimated that only a small number of the boys subjected to the mutilation survived after the surgery.

When American colonists rebelled against British rule in 1776, American merchant ships lost Royal Navy protection. With no American Navy for protection, American ships were attacked and their Christian crews enslaved by Muslim pirates operating under the control of the "Dey of Algiers"--an Islamist warlord ruling Algeria.

Because American commerce in the Mediterranean was being destroyed by the pirates, the Continental Congress agreed in 1784 to negotiate treaties with the four Barbary States. Congress appointed a special commission consisting of John Adams, Thomas Jefferson, and Benjamin Franklin, to oversee the negotiations.

Lacking the ability to protect its merchant ships in the Mediterranean, the new America government tried to appease the Muslim slavers by agreeing to pay tribute and ransoms in order to retrieve seized American ships and buy the freedom of enslaved sailors.

Adams argued in favor of paying tribute as the cheapest way to get American commerce in the Mediterranean moving again. Jefferson was opposed. He believed there would be no end to the demands for tribute and wanted matters settled "through the medium of war." He proposed a league of trading nations to force an end to Muslim piracy.

In 1786, Jefferson, then the American ambassador to France, and Adams, then the American ambassador to Britain, met in London with Sidi Haji Abdul Rahman Adja, the "Dey of Algiers" ambassador to Britain.

The Americans wanted to negotiate a peace treaty based on Congress' vote to appease.

During the meeting Jefferson and Adams asked the Dey's ambassador why Muslims held so much hostility towards America, a nation with which they had no previous contacts.

In a later meeting with the American Congress, the two future presidents reported that Ambassador Sidi Haji Abdul Rahman Adja had answered that Islam "was founded on the Laws of their Prophet, that it was written in their Quran, that all nations who should not *have acknowledged their authority were sinners, that it was their right and duty to make war upon them wherever they could be found, and to make slaves of all they could take as Prisoners, and that every Musselman (Muslim) who should be slain in Battle was sure to go to Paradise."*

For the following 15 years, the American government paid the Muslims millions of dollars for the safe passage of American ships or the return of American hostages. The payments in ransom and tribute amounted to 20 percent of United States government annual revenues in 1800.

Not long after Jefferson's inauguration as president in 1801, he dispatched a group of frigates to defend American interests in the Mediterranean, and informed Congress.

Declaring that America was going to spend "millions for defense but not one cent for tribute," Jefferson pressed the issue by deploying American Marines and many of America's best warships to the Muslim Barbary Coast.

The USS Constitution, USS Constellation, USS Philadelphia, USS Chesapeake, USS Argus, USS Syren and USS Intrepid all saw action.

In 1805, American Marines marched across the desert from Egypt into Tripolitania, forcing the surrender of Tripoli and the freeing of all American slaves.

During the Jefferson administration, the Muslim Barbary States, crumbling as a result of intense American naval bombardment and on shore raids by Marines, finally officially agreed to abandon slavery and piracy.

Jefferson's victory over the Muslims lives on today in the Marine Hymn, with the line, "From the halls of Montezuma, to the shores of Tripoli, We fight our country's battles in the air, on land and sea."

It wasn't until 1815 that the problem was fully settled by the total defeat of all the Muslim slave trading pirates.

Jefferson had been right. The "medium of war" was the only way to put an end to the Muslim problem.
www.usvetdsp.com/jan07/jeff_quran.htm

John Quincy Adams, our sixth President writing in 1830:

In the seventh century of the Christian era, a wandering Arab of the lineage of Hagar, the Egyptian, combining the powers of transcendent genius, with the preternatural energy of a fanatic, and the fraudulent spirit of an impostor, proclaimed himself as a messenger from Heaven, and spread desolation and delusion over an extensive portion of the earth. Adopting from the sublime conception of the Mosaic Law, the doctrine of one omnipotent God, he connected indissolubly with it, the audacious falsehood, that he was himself his prophet and apostle.

Adopting from the new Revelation of Jesus, the faith and hope of immortal life, and of future retribution, he humbled it to the dust, by adapting all the rewards and sanctions of his religion to the gratification of the sexual passion. He poisoned the sources of human felicity at the fountain, by degrading the condition the female sex, and the allowance of polygamy, and he declared undistinguishing and exterminating war, as a part of his religion, against all the rest of mankind. THE ESSENCE OF HIS DOCTRINE WAS VIOLENCE AND LUST: TO EXALT THE BRUTAL OVER THE SPRITIUAL PART OF HUMAN NATURE.

*Between these two religions, thus contrasted in their characters, a war of twelve hundred years has already raged. That war is yet flagrant; nor can it cease but by the extinction of that imposture which has been permitted by Providence to prolong the degeneracy of man. While the merciless and dissolute dogmas of the false prophet shall furnish motives to human action, there can never be peace upon earth, and good will towards men. The hand of Ismael will be against every man, and every man's hand against him. It is, indeed, amongst the mysterious dealings of God, that this delusion should have been suffered for so many ages, and during so many generations of human kind, to prevail over the doctrines of the meek and peaceful and benevolent Jesus (Blunt, 1830, 29:269, capitals in orig.)*Source:apologeticspress.org/apcontent.aspx?category=7&article=1142

The Reason for founding the United States Navy

The first full time, fully equipped US Navy was established by Congress in 1794 with the express purpose of defeating the Islamic Barbary pirates. Eleven years earlier, two normal ships had been used briefly in the Revolutionary War and then disbanded. The Navy uses the earliest date as it birth, but the 1794 Naval Act was the official Congressional authorization. http://en.wikipedia.org/wiki/Naval_Act_of_1794

Fast forward to the 21st Century and we see the same phenomena with the Somali pirates at the other end of the African continent. **223 ships** were captured or attacked off the Somali coast from 2005-2012, a period of only eight years. Source: http://en.wikipedia.org/wiki/List_of_ships_attacked_by_Somali_pira tes

Islam has not changed. In fact, it has become emboldened with the continued rise of the terrorist groups and perceived victories in Iraq and Afghanistan. The Arab Spring that began in 2011 has brought the Muslim Brotherhood to power in several Mid-East nations, further fanning the flames of jihad. Egypt and Syria's troubles appear to have only just begun. Isaiah seems to have had a prophetic vision of the Arab Spring in Isaiah 19. Reading that chapter is like reading the latest news, only it is more accurate. The good news is that it ends with Egypt's salvation by Yehovah, God of Israel, Who reveals their Savior.

YEHOVAH IS FAITHFUL!

Chapter 10 - Where the Domino Theory Ends

Middle East Dominoes was the subject of my January 16, 2011 commentary. We have seen the dominoes fall at a dizzying pace. Where will it lead? Where will it stop? The final result will be the resurrection of the Islamic Caliphate. The entire Islamic Empire will be revived from Indonesia to Morocco; and from Turkey and the "stans" to the Sudan and Somalia. This will transpire in just a few years.

How can such a monumental event occur so fast? There are two forces, one physical, one spiritual. The physical is the brute force of revolution and is well under way in Gaza, Tunisia, Libya, Egypt, Yemen, Syria, Lebanon and even Jordan. It will continue to amplify until the fall of the Arab world to radical Islam and the revived Caliphate.

The second force is spiritual. Radical Islam is above all else a spiritual movement. (Radicals, fundamentalists or Islamists are simply Muslims who follow the fundamental core of Islam from the Quran, Sunnah and Hadiths. The other Muslims, no matter how large a percentage, are considered apostate by the Islamists). The spiritual component makes it a political ideology on demonic steroids. If Communism was not godless it may have conquered the world. Ideas alone are not enough. But ideas with fanatical allegiance to an apocalyptic deity will indeed threaten the entire world. Now couple these facts with the Biblical narrative.

> *Then He charged them, saying, "Take heed, beware of the leaven of the Pharisees and the leaven of Herod."*
> Mark 8:15

Jesus warned against the leaven of the Pharisees **and** of Herod. The Pharisees had a religious spirit which rules by self-righteousness. Herod had a political spirit which rules by self-interest. Islam is more dangerous than Communism because it embraces both demonic principalities.

Psalm 83 is also a core prophecy that must be understood. I have been speaking and writing about it for several years. The first five verses explain the motive of these enemies: hatred of the God of the Bible who is worshipped by both Christians and Jews. Since God is out of reach, they must indirectly attack His chosen people Israel, even to the extent "that the name of Israel be remembered no more."

> *Do not keep silent, O God! Do not hold your peace, and do not be still, O God! For behold, your enemies make a tumult; and those who hate you have lifted up their head. They have taken crafty counsel against your people, and consulted together against your sheltered ones. They have said, "Come, and let us cut them off from being a nation, that the name of Israel may be remembered no more." For they have consulted together with one consent; they form a confederacy against you.* (Psalm 83:1-5)

The Psalm continues by listing the actual attacking countries. The prophecy stands alone, but is even more profound when compared with a more common prophecy of the Gog and Magog War recorded in Ezekiel 38. This later war also lists the countries involved. The amazing fact is that none of the Psalm 83 protagonist countries are listed in Ezekiel's prophecy. This leads to the conclusion that Israel actually wins the Psalm 83 war and occupies much of the surrounding territory. The first Israel land promise to Abraham was *"from the river of Egypt to the great river Euphrates"* (Genesis 15:18)

Another distinction between the prophecies is that the Psalm 83 nations in the closer ring around the land of Israel are all Arab Muslim nations. The nations remaining are mostly non-Arab Muslims. It is this larger circle of nations that fulfills the Biblical antichrist prophecies. The Islamic Empire will rise again and be governed under Sharia Law by the Caliphate. This revived empire will be ruled by the Islamic messianic figure called the Mahdi (or Twelfth Imam).

My friend Walid Shoebat, an ex-Muslim and former terrorist, expressed the process clearly in his excellent book: God's War on Terror: Islam, Prophecy and the Bible.

> *"Biblically, the Empire of the Antichrist will not be a new empire; rather it will be the revival of a previously great empire that will have suffered what the Bible calls a 'fatal head wound'. (Revelation 13:3) But the wound will be healed and the empire will be revived from the dead as it were: 'And the beast [Antichrist Empire] which I saw was like a leopard, and his feet were like those of a bear, and his mouth like the mouth of a lion. And the dragon gave him his power and his*

throne and great authority. And I saw one of his heads as if it had been slain and his fatal wound healed. And the whole world was amazed and followed after the beast." (Revelation 13:2-3) *"Today the Caliphate exists only in the desires of hundreds of millions of Muslims worldwide who want to revive this beast that was slain March 3, 1924. The last Caliphate – the Ottoman Caliphate – was officially abolished by the first President of the Turkish Republic, Mustafa Kemal Ataturk. The abolition of the Caliphate is profoundly significant for our study. For it was on this day that the Islamic Empire, led by a sitting Caliph for over fourteen hundred years suffered a fatal head wound. The position of "head of state" of the Islamic Empire was severed."* Walid Shoebat with Joel Richardson, God's War on Terror (Top Executive Media 2008) p.81

The part that jumps out in Walid's quote is the interpretation of the fatal head wound. By applying that verse to the line of Caliphs, we come full circle to our conclusion. The Middle East dominoes are falling. It is now unstoppable until the rise of the final Caliph and his Caliphate over the Muslim world and however many other nations that succumb to Islamic dominance. Ignorance and apathy are blinding many from this truth. It is time for the West to open their eyes to the inevitable realities. It is time to wake up, stand up and speak up!

Unfortunately, the response in the US and the Western world seems to be: "Hear no evil, speak no evil, see no evil." In the official 9-11 Report, the frequency of the words "Islam",

"Sharia", "Jihad", "Muslim", "Hamas" and "Hezbollah" totaled over 600. Yet in three subsequent documents (The National Intelligence Strategy, an FBI Counter Terrorism Document, and The Ft. Hood Report) the total word count of those specific words in each, is ZERO! While it could be argued that "political correctness" could have somewhat reduced the 600 word count to a lower number; the absolute elimination of these words in three separate documents cannot be explained by simple political correctness. Our present Administration is intentionally censoring the very words that explain the true source of today's terror.

Yet, all these things are clearly foretold in the Bible. What a day to be alive! As I said in the Overview, this does not need to be unnecessarily complex. I have tried to keep it simple and useful. Now that we have an idea of the force that is facing our generation, we need some practical action items. What can we do about it? We are certainly not helpless. As with Queen Esther, perhaps Yehovah has brought us into the Kingdom for such a time as this. God is with us. Let's roll up our sleeves and get to work.

YEHOVAH IS FAITHFUL!

Part IV: Action Items

Chapter 11 - Stop Saying the Names of other gods

Most God-fearing Christians and Jews completely understand and respect the first commandment to have "no other gods" before Yehovah. Yet, in the Western nations, including America, many have opened up their thinking to other gods in the name of tolerance. This makes me want to ask them: "What part of 'no other gods' don't you understand?"

It is only recently that I have found a more specific prohibition on the subject. You may have noticed by now that I am reluctant to say or write the name of the god of Islam. It is because the Bible prohibits it! What if we in America or at least believers were to practice the following four scriptures? Notice how the Holy Spirit progressively adds another component to the prohibition with each verse.

Here is the prohibition

> And in all that I have said to you, be circumspect and make no mention of the name of other gods, nor let it be heard from your mouth (Exodus 23:13).

Then Joshua adds three more conditions.

> You shall not make mention of the name of their gods, nor cause anyone to swear by them; you shall not serve them nor bow down to them, but you shall

hold fast to Yehovah your God, as you have done to this day (Joshua 23:7).

The way a person converts to Islam is by standing in a public place and swearing allegiance three times to the god of Islam and his messenger, Muhammad. The next step is to serve that god and bow down to it. You have seen many examples of Muslims doing that even in public five times a day. I am ashamed to say that in a widely publicized picture, President Obama, who professes Christianity, bowed down 90 degrees from the waist to the King of Saudi Arabia, who is the religious custodian/keeper of Mecca.

The third scripture introduces another aspect, blood, which especially applies to Islam. This blood thirsty death cult delights in the shedding of blood in the name of their god. Hence, we hear the perverse oath proclaimed by every suicide bomber before detonation, that his god is the greatest.

Their sorrows shall be multiplied who hasten after another god; Their drink offerings of blood I will not offer, nor take up their names on my lips (Psalm 16:4).

Fourth, Hosea adds a final point. Not only will we not speak their names, but eventually their names will not even be remembered.

For I will take from her mouth the names of the Baals, and they shall be remembered by their name no more (Hosea 2:17).

Psalm 83:4 highlights an amazing contrast: *They have said, "Come, and let us cut them off from being a nation, that the name of Israel may be remembered no more."* Satan does not have an original creative thought in his head. He can only twist and pervert what God says or does. So his plan to remove the remembrance of Israel is nothing more than a copycat idea from the truth that the devil and all his false gods face in eternity.

> *Now therefore, fear Yehovah, serve Him in sincerity and in truth, and put away the gods which your fathers served on the other side of the River and in Egypt. Serve Yehovah!* (Joshua 24:14)

We have already been lulled into complacency by using the name of the top pagan goddess, called Ishtar in Babylon and known by other names in other cultures. Christians use her name in place of Resurrection Day, calling it by her name, Easter, which is a derivative of the Babylonian "queen of heaven". To top off the deception, King James Bible translators even miss-translate Acts 12:1 using the name of the goddess instead of Passover, which is the real word in the Greek (Pesach). Most translations have corrected this error, but it is still used almost universally by Christians. Is it that important to correct this error? I am convinced that it is critical, along with using God's personal name, Yehovah. Only Satan and Allah benefit from our ignorance.

Elijah and the name of Yehovah

We all love the account of Elijah on Mt. Carmel doing battle with the prophets of Baal. Yet, have you considered this story in regards to God's name? Elijah sets the parameters clearly on God's name.

*"Then you call on the **name** of your gods, and I will call on the **name** of Yehovah; and the God who answers by fire, He is God." So all the people answered and said, "It is well spoken."* 1 Kings 18:24

When God answered with fire and revealed His power, the people knew exactly what it meant.

*Now when all the people saw it, they fell on their faces; and they said, **"Yehovah, He is God! Yehovah, He is God!"*** 1 Kings 18:38

(Please excuse my frustration, but it so silly to change the specific personal name of Yehovah for the generic LORD in these verses as most translators wrongly do.)

Isn't it about time that we line up with the Scriptures? It is now more important than ever with the pagan Islamic threat to our entire Judeo-Christian culture. Let's start using the personal name of our God, Yehovah and just stop saying the names of other gods, especially the god of Islam.

YEHOVAH IS FAITHFUL!

Chapter 12 - Help Muslims Become Ex-Muslims

Perhaps the most important point in this entire book is the distinction between Yehovah God of Israel, and A-la, the god of Islam. Yehovah is the God of Abraham, Isaac and Jacob. He is the God of the Bible who is the eternal Father. The god of Islam is not a father and has no son. Yet, there are some folks who say a Muslim can accept Jesus and remain a Muslim. That is wrong. There are two errors here.

Error #1: The first and most obvious is confusion over thinking we all worship the same God. I have made this point emphatically. So, Islam is paganism. Therefore when one finds the true God he leaves his other gods behind. A Muslim becomes a former Muslim. This is also true for Gentiles who find salvation in the Son of God. We become former Gentiles. The Apostle Paul makes this point.

You know that you were Gentiles, carried away to these dumb idols, however you were led. 1 Corinthians 12:2

Therefore remember that you, once Gentiles in the flesh, who are called Uncircumcision by what is called the Circumcision made in the flesh by hand, that at that time you were without Christ, being aliens from the commonwealth of Israel and strangers from the covenants of promise, having no hope and without God in the world. But now in Christ Jesus you who once were far off have been brought near by the blood of Christ.

*Now, therefore, you are no longer strangers and foreigners, but **fellow citizens** with the saints and **members of the household of God**, Ephesians 2:11-13, 19*

It may be a little picky, but I consider myself an ex-Gentile, now that I have been grafted into the commonwealth of Israel. Hallelujah!

Error #2: The second error of those who think a Muslim can remain a Muslim is the error of race. Islam is not a race. It is a religious and political system. Defenders of Islam have quite successfully claimed Islamophobia. They insist that they are targeted for violence and discrimination simply because they are Muslim as if it were a racial issue. Here is a statistical analysis of hate crimes against Muslims in America since 9/11.

> *As the usual voices fault "our oversaturated Islamophobic environment" and "growing anti-Muslim hate," they neglect to mention how rare it is for an actual or perceived Muslim to die in a hate crime. By the FBI's count, 74 people were killed in hate crimes ("murder and nonnegligent manslaughter" in Table 4) from 2002 to 2011, but **not a single one in an anti-Muslim incident. Indeed, the FBI lists no anti-Muslim fatalities since 1995,** corresponding to the earliest report available.* (Hate-Crime Stats Deflate 'Islamophobia' Myth by David Rusin. National Review 1-11-13)

Islamophobia means "fear of Islam". It is those who are giving in to Islamic pressure that cower in fear. Those of us who speak out and stand against the Islamic agenda are not afraid. The truth is that Islam is afraid and hates the God of Abraham, Isaac and Jacob.

So, there are Muslims of every race and most nationalities. When an Arab Muslim comes to Christ, he is still an Arab, but not a Muslim. When an Iranian Muslim becomes a believer in the Jesus of the Bible, he is still an Iranian, but is then an ex-Muslim. The same is true for Indonesian Muslims or American or Chinese or any other nationality or race. A Hindu who accepts Jesus becomes an ex-Hindu. A Buddhist becomes an ex-Buddhist; an atheist becomes an ex-atheist. You get the picture. So the glorious news is that in Jesus, we all become one and **are grafted** into Israel which the Bible calls "the cultivated olive tree". Even Israel, who in times past turned away from Yehovah, will turn back to Him and be restored. We former Gentiles are the "wild olive tree" in this quote.

For if you were cut out of the olive tree which is wild by nature, and were grafted contrary to nature into a cultivated olive tree, how much more will these, who are natural branches, be grafted into their own olive tree?
Romans 11:24

YEHOVAH IS FAITHFUL!

Chapter 13 - Invite Jesus into Muslim Hearts

My last goal of this book is to offer the grace of Yehovah God in Jesus to every Muslim who is searching for Truth. Please consider inviting Jesus into your heart, just as you would invite someone into your home in hospitality. Then after you have considered all of His claims, invite Him to be the owner of your heart. Yield to Him in an intentional act of voluntary submission to the Lord of Life!

Are Muslims too far gone for salvation? Of course not! Muslims can be saved the same way we all can. When God revealed His love for the "world" in John 3:16 there were not any exceptions. Even when God has to judge the wicked, He does not rejoice but grieves that they have rejected Him, His Son, and His Plan. Yehovah, the God of Israel did not even celebrate the death of Osama bin Laden according to the Bible:

> "For I have no pleasure in the death of one who dies," says the Lord Yehovah. "Therefore turn and live!" Ezekiel 18:32

Back in the Jesus movement of the 1960's and 70's, lots of Hippies were finding Jesus. However, not all found salvation. Some just added Jesus to all their other motley beliefs. But many turned away from all their past false beliefs and embraced Jesus as the Messiah, Son of God and the only way to God the Father. Jesus Himself left no doubt about His claims. He was either who He claimed to be or the worst false prophet in history.

> *Jesus said to him,* "I am the way, the truth, and the life. No one comes to the Father except through Me. If you had known Me, you would have known My Father also; and from now on you know Him and have seen Him." John 14:6-7

When you talk to Muslims about Jesus, they already understand the simple confession to convert to Islam. A convert must simply say publicly that the god of Islam is the only god and Muhammad is his prophet. So, on the other hand, converting out of Islam to Biblical faith in Jesus, is likewise a simple confession.

> *But what does it say? "The word is near you, in your mouth and in your heart" (that is, the word of faith which we preach): that **if you confess with your mouth the Lord Jesus and believe in your heart that God has raised Him from the dead, you will be saved.** For with the heart one believes unto righteousness, and with the mouth confession is made unto salvation.* Romans 10:8-10

One simply needs to sincerely believe and declare that Jesus is the savior through the blood of His death and resurrection, and that Yehovah is the true God and Father.

Muslims are enslaved to sin as we all are without Jesus, but Muslims are also slaves to their god. They are commanded to bow five times a day and their entire lives are dominated by

Sharia. They are slaves. Christians, on the other hand, used to be slaves to sin but are now set free in Jesus! Instead of bowing as the conquered enemy of God we are made part of His family and stand as free men in liberty.

> *I desire therefore that the men pray everywhere, **lifting up holy hands**, without wrath and doubting;* 1 Timothy 2:8

> ***Therefore if the Son makes you free, you shall be free indeed.*** John 8:36

> ***Stand fast*** *therefore in the **liberty** by which Christ has made us free, and do not be entangled again with a yoke of bondage.* Galatians 5:1

> *Therefore take up the whole armor of God that you may be able to withstand in the evil day, and having done all, **to stand. Stand therefore,** having girded your waist with truth, having put on the breastplate of righteousness.* Ephesians 6:13-14

Muslims also come with an understanding of submission. The name Muslim means: one who submits. The joyful difference is that where submission to Islam is demanded and imposed, yielding to Jesus is completely voluntary. It is a choice of liberty, from the free will granted to us by our Heavenly Father.

> *I call heaven and earth as witnesses today against you, that I have set before you life and death, blessing and cursing; therefore choose life, that both you and your*

descendants may live; that you may love Yehovah your God. Deuteronomy 30:19-20

So, a Muslim repents of his sins just like we all do, and turns from the false god with a totally new lifestyle of righteousness, peace and joy in the Holy Spirit.

*For the kingdom of God is not eating and drinking, but righteousness and peace and joy in the Holy Spirit. For he who serves Christ in these things is **acceptable to God** and approved by men.* Romans 14:17-18

A new believer who is a former Muslim will also want to be immersed in water baptism as a sign of his transformation from death to life. Being baptized declares to the world that you have died with Jesus in His death and have been raised from the death of sin to a brand new life with all sins forgiven!

*What shall we say then? Shall we continue in sin that grace may abound? Certainly not! How shall we who died to sin live any longer in it? Or do you not know that as many of us as were baptized into Christ Jesus were baptized into His death? Therefore **we were buried with Him through baptism into death,** that just as Christ was raised from the dead by the glory of the Father, even so we also should walk in newness of life.* Romans 6:1-4

We also need to share the wonderful power to live the Jesus life that He provides in the baptism of the Holy Spirit. First, we are baptized into Jesus and salvation by the Holy Spirit, and then we are baptized into the Holy Spirit and power by Jesus. Both of these baptisms are provided for all believers.

> *The next day John saw Jesus coming toward him, and said, "Behold! The Lamb of God who takes away the sin of the world! This is He of whom I said, 'After me comes a Man who is preferred before me, for He was before me.' I did not know Him; but that He should be revealed to Israel, therefore I came baptizing with water." And John bore witness, saying, "I saw the Spirit descending from heaven like a dove, and He remained upon Him. I did not know Him, but He who sent me to baptize with water said to me, 'Upon whom you see the Spirit descending, and remaining on Him, **this is He who baptizes with the Holy Spirit.**' And I have seen and testified that this is the Son of God."* John 1:29-34

Another very important transformation happens by your own choice of conduct. A great friend of mine, Dr. Jay Swallow, is a Native American apostle and the Chief of the Cheyenne Indian Nation. He taught me something profound about protocol when dealing with demonic forces. This is necessary for new believers to make a total break from their past contact with evil spirits. Jay explained that removing the old authority is an act of taking off the mantle of authority from the old way and placing all the authority with Jesus. An example is the cape that is put on a college graduate representing his degree. If he were for some reason to forfeit his degree, the mantle would be removed. That is exactly what we are doing. We are "dismantling" the old nature and giving all authority to Jesus. We become a new man in Him!

95

*As the truth is in Jesus: that you **put off, concerning your former conduct, the old man** which grows corrupt according to the deceitful lusts, and be renewed in the spirit of your mind, and that **you put on the new man** which was created according to God, in true righteousness and holiness.* Ephesians 4:21-24

A Final Word to Christians

We have flown over 1,400 years of Islam. We observed their actions and the responses of other nations, often ending in wars and death. But we must remember that we have a superior warfare. Ours is not with human effort and military battles, but with the supernatural power of Yehovah God through Jesus.

For though we walk in the flesh, we do not war according to the flesh. For the weapons of our warfare are not carnal but mighty in God for pulling down strongholds. 2 Corinthians 10:3-4

For we are not fighting against flesh-and-blood enemies, but against evil rulers and authorities of the unseen world, against mighty powers in this dark world, and against evil spirits in the heavenly places. Ephesians 6:12 NLT

Let us all agree to intercede together in prayer for the salvation of Muslims all over the earth. May Yehovah God Himself, in mercy, grant the revelation of His Son, Yeshua ben Yehovah to all who love Truth and who hunger and thirst for righteousness.

YEHOVAH IS FAITHFUL!